MAN WITH

AN

ATTITUDE

Acknowledgments

I am in great debt to Dennis Carpenter, Charlie Hedrick, Greg Jenks, Kris and Katherine Komarnitsky, and Robert Miller for providing suggestions which improved both the format and content of this handbook, resulting in an increase of clarity and ease of use. A special thank you to my wife Eileen for advice on the selection of a cover design which we see as a view from the shoreline of Lake Galilee as the sun rises in the midst of cloud formations, with a storm possibly forming on the horizon. Of course, any mistakes and shortcomings in the development of the book are strictly my own.

Endorsements and Praise for this Book

Dennis Dean Carpenter, Educator and Author
"This excellent biblical study offers a different perspective, and it includes a reader response strategy for understanding the relevance of Jesus the man. Once begun, no reader can escape reflecting on how to be a human being."

Elizabeth Holmes, St. Louis Missouri
"Everyone wants to make his or her life count. In a careful, thought provoking way, Stecher's book urges us to be the message of Jesus as living examples in our communities of embracing the attitudes that shaped his outreach to others."

Gregory C. Jenks, Biblical Scholar and Priest
"Stecher gives us a helpful way to approach the life of Jesus. Paying attention to attitudes which Jesus advocated and practiced offers a fresh entry point for people seeking to draw on his legacy for their own lives today. A useful handbook for both religious and non-religious alike."

Kris Komarnitsky, Airline Pilot
"Drawing on the findings of the Jesus Seminar, Stecher's attitudes compilation is the most compact portrait of Jesus of which I am aware, and it leaves the reader with eight indisputably great principles to live by."

Robert J. Miller, Professor of Religious Studies, Juniata College
"The idea of reconstructing attitudes from sayings is an interesting way to try to organize a disparate body of materials into coherent themes that afford us a helpful way to understand the historical Jesus (Jesus the man)."

Mike Short, Philosopher of Science
"Stecher has a unique perspective and a fresh approach, using Jesus' attitudes to develop a distinct image of Jesus the man. The reader can't help thinking about his/her own attitudes. This book can be a faith building tool, and it will be a terrific resource for personal or group study."

Man With An Attitude: A Handbook of Life Challenges From the Jesus Story

A Personal Growth and Parenting Guide

Eugene Stecher

Man With An Attitude: A Handbook of Life Challenges From the Jesus Story. Copyright 2020 by Eugene H. Stecher. Printed in the United States of America. The author gives permission for parts of this handbook to be reproduced, as needed, in educational and worship settings. Otherwise, except for brief quotations, this handbook may not be reproduced in any manner without prior written permission by the author. Inquiries can be sent to **stecher@pa.net**. Any evaluative comments, both positive and negative, are welcome and can be sent to the same address. All royalties will be used for promotion and distribution.

Biblical quotes are taken from the "New Revised Standard Version Bible: Catholic Edition, copyright 1993 by the Division of Christian Education of the National Council of Churches of Christ in the U.S.A. Used by permission. All rights reserved." Quotes from the *Gospel of Thomas* are taken from the public domain translation of Mark M. Mattison found at https://www.gospels.net/thomas/. Significant differences in wording with the Jesus Seminar's *The Complete Gospels: The Scholars' Version* (2010) translation of the Gospels are noted throughout the text. Chapter three of this Handbook is an expanded version of the article, "Man With an Attitude," which appeared in *The FourthR*, 32:5, September-October (2019). Permission to use the article has been granted by Robert J. Miller, Ed.

Kindle Direct Publishing
ISBN: 9798667593850

This book is a thank you to those who are willing to pay attention to the humanity of Jesus of Nazareth

Table of Contents

Preparation

Having a good laugh with Jesus..9

Methodology and Purpose...10

Research Tool: What did Jesus do?..17

Attitudes

One: Make your life count...21

Two: Practice goal-oriented passion..29

Three: Be other-centered in relationships.................................38

Four: Encourage the powerless..46

Five: Use your money for unselfish purposes............................52

Six: Be flexible in the use of tradition...57

Seven: Replace anxiety with trust...64

Eight: Take on outreach responsibility.......................................69

Reflection

Looking Forward...74

Appendix One: Summary of Attitudes..77

Appendix Two: Questions for Discussion..82

Sources

Bibliography...86

End Notes...88

Having a Good Laugh with Jesus

The term, "handbook", sometimes referred to as a vade mecum (Latin, "go with me") or pocket reference* is defined by the American Heritage Dictionary in two ways:

First, the handbook is "a concise manual or reference book providing specific information or instruction about a subject." In other words, a handbook teaches a skill set in a particular area of expertise. It could be, for example, a skill set for repairing an automobile. In the present case the skill set is the attitudes for living revealed in the teachings and actions of Jesus.

Second, the handbook is "a book in which off-track bets are recorded." I suggest that our unique source Jesus, as the reader shall see, was a master at producing verbal paintings of visual contrasts that were humorous, challenging, and even troubling and shocking, and would himself now be laughing and perhaps saying, "How ironic is that!", as he visualized the contrast between the life changing potential of his attitudes and the promise of an off-track bet.

As I write this, America has concluded a six day mourning and celebratory remembrance of congressman John Robert Lewis, the civil rights leader who championed equality for all and was especially active in the equal voting rights movement of the 1960s. He was famous for the concept "good trouble" to which he challenged others to devote their lives. When I consider the life, teachings, and attitudes of Jesus, I can think of no better phrase to describe his behavior than "good trouble."

*https://en.wikipedia.org/wiki/Handbook.

Methodology and Purpose

Methodology: Searching for the Attitudes of Jesus.

The historical memory of someone may be more accurately described as imitating his or her personal attitudes, rather than recalling specific events, words, or actions. Those with expertise in psychology and psychiatry define an attitude as follows:

"a relatively stable disposition or readiness to react in a specific way to a person, group, idea, or situation. Attitudes are complex products of learning, experience, and emotional processes and include, e.g., our enduring preferences, prejudices, superstitions, scientific or religious views, and political predilections and aversions."[1]

I understand an attitude to be a consistent way of living, a predictable mindset, being disposed to a habitual inclination or tendency in a certain set of circumstances. In other words, attitude refers to a pattern of feeling-speaking-acting, a reliably repeated reaction in similar circumstances in a variety of times and places.

For example, six to seven decades ago my father said to my brother and me as young children, something like, "I hope you boys never smoke or drink." We both took that seriously because that one moment simply represented the attitude throughout his life that it is a mistake to put harmful substances into one's body. I then did my best to model that attitude into the next generation, and of course that included keeping a much wider range of harmful and illegal substances out of one's body. And then the next generation followed with their own adaptation of the attitude. Something similar about the staying power of attitude could also be said about my mother's approach to higher education for her children, as carried forward by myself and my children, but in that instance no memory at all survives of any specific words that she might have said.

As applied to the authentic Jesus of history, J. D. Crossan writes of the attitude concept as follows:

"I would vote positively for the saying usually translated as 'Blessed are the poor,' but I can never be certain whether it recalls an aphorism (a wise teaching*) or summarizes an attitude of Jesus. That second possibility is even more secure than the former, especially for those living by a similar attitude. Once again for emphasis: The continuity between Jesus and his first companions is less in memory than in mimesis, less in remembrance than in imitation."[2]

*This clarification is not in the original material.

It seems reasonable to assume that a strong belief in the soon return of the risen Christ* delayed the writing down of biographical material following Jesus' death. For example, the Apostle Paul asserted: "You know what time it is, how it is now the moment for you to wake from sleep. For salvation is nearer to us now than when we first became believers; the night is far gone, the day is near (. . .)." (Romans 13:11–12). The date estimate for Paul's conversion to the risen Christ falls between 31 and 35 CE. The estimated dating for the Pauline letters is 51–57 CE.[3] The most frequently estimated date for the earliest gospel, Mark, is "about the time of the Roman-Judaean war 66–70 CE."[4]

*This expression represents Jesus' after death identity according to believers.

Also, the oral culture, i.e., the reliance on preserving oral discourse in memory among the early first century Palestinian peasantry, certainly was an additional factor that initially contributed to a delay in written material.[5] Scholars generally agree that oral memories would have had to survive the pressure of change for at least two decades following Jesus death.[6]

Given these factors, the primary authentic component of this early church material was probably Jesus' attitudes rather than a precise memory of words or actions. It seems best to assume that, from the beginning, at least some followers were inspired to repeat what they experienced as attitudes, as consistencies in his behavior.

To determine Jesus' attitudes, I've used what the Jesus Seminar identified as the authentic historical teachings and events. Across the centuries biblical scholarship had taken the form of the writings and interpretations of brilliant individuals. For the first time in history scholars were brought together from across the country and voted as a group on what was considered authentic to Jesus. They basically used four categories: certainty, probability, possibility, definitely not. The Jesus Seminar's work constitutes a massive effort:

"It is the collective report of gospel scholars working closely together for six years (. . .). They first of all inventoried all the surviving ancient texts for words attributed to Jesus (. . .). They produced a translation known as the Scholar's Version. And, finally, they studied, debated, and voted on each of the more than 1,500 sayings of Jesus in the inventory."[7]

The Seminar thought of its vote as "the core or gist" of how Jesus presented himself.[8] When looking at the word pictures that his self-presentation inspired, what comes to mind are concrete and vivid creations of contrasts, exaggeration, humor, paradox, irony, metaphor, and the like. The Seminar was most impressed by material that challenged common social and religious views, and tended to be "dissimilar" from the emphases of the gospel writers. If there was support from at least two independent sources that raised confidence in authenticity.[9] Another confidence booster was a finding of consistency between words and actions.[10] The primary sources used by the Seminar were the four gospels of the early Christian movement: Matthew, Mark, Luke, and John, as well as the Gospel of Thomas which was part of the archeological discoveries at Nag Hamadi, Egypt in 1945.

Others have made suggestions, but I take full responsibility for the derivation of attitudes from this authentic material. The author's role is the interpretation, organization, and clarification of the material according to the types of attitudes in evidence. My method was to gather together similar meanings into complexes across multiple teachings, stories, and events. Other persons or groups looking at the same material might have different ideas about what should be emphasized and about how the final product should be worded. Perhaps, not surprisingly, the reader may conclude that an individual teaching, story, or event may be relatively confidently placed under multiple attitude headings. My goal has been to handle the following dynamics effectively when assigning authentic material to an attitude complex:

Briefly worded material. These verses often provide few or no internal clues as to what is to be imitated. We are left wondering, for example, what is the "narrow door" and the "fire cast upon the world," and the "nothing" that some will have "taken away," and what is "hidden to be revealed," and to what does "wise as serpents," and "innocent as doves" refer. The assignment of such material to an attitude complex is arguably an educated guess, at best.

Contexts provided by the gospel writers. These contexts complicate matters because they frequently seem prejudiced toward the concerns of the early Christian movement, rather than being reflective of the life circumstances of Jesus. For example, the parable of the son who squandered his inheritance immediately follows an observation about rejoicing over one sinner who repents, but the story actually seems to be about the complicated relationships of a father and two sons.

Material of greater length. Generally, these verses seem to be more transparent about a possible attitude. For example, the story in which the workers receive equal pay for unequal hours seems likely to be supporting the attitude that God's way does not make decisions by means of society's standards.

Purpose: What are the attractions of the attitude approach?

General populace. Attitudes provide a much shorter written narrative of the historical Jesus. Pages of teachings/actions, for example, might be reduced to a single paragraph. This factor may pique the interest of some persons in this category. Also, the eight basic life challenges would seem to be an excellent personal growth resource as well as a teaching tool for parenting children of all ages.

Christian laity and pastors. In addition to the general population personal growth and parenting factors, I would argue that the attitude approach is certainly also a major advancement for the Christian layperson and pastor, both of whom might view the essential Jesus as more accessible when condensed into a comparatively few pages. Accessibility means that the "make your life count" message could compete more effectively with Easter's "faith for eternal life message." The common denominator is liberation: the first from an unproductive life, the second from death. Rather than having information about the Jesus of history overwhelmed by the Christ eternal life story, maybe we would get more balance in the form of hearing more sermons and Christian education lessons on the essential Jesus and having more interest in adapting Jesus' attitudes to our own lives. Perhaps it would be of lasting value for children to memorize the eight basic attitudes of the human Jesus in the same manner as they might memorize a Boy Scout or Girl Scout creed.

Scholars' community. The benefit for scholars of studying attitudes is the opportunity to discuss and apply another tool as they continue the search for authentic historical Jesus material in the gospels. Might we see another group like the Jesus Seminar formed to vote on which material in the gospels represents authentic attitudes?

Reader Response Notes:

Reader Response Notes:

REFERENCE TOOL: WHAT DID JESUS DO?

The Votes of the Jesus Seminar[11]

In order to provide context for the attitudes that will be explored in the main section of the handbook, this section summarizes the activity of Jesus in terms of what actions seem certain or probable. The scriptural citations are representative but not all inclusive.

Jesus was a descendent of Abraham (Matthew 1:1). He was born to a woman named Mary, probably during the reign of Herod the Great (Luke 2:5–6). He was likely circumcised and named on the eighth day as per Jewish custom (Luke 2:21). He was known as the son of Joseph (Luke 3:23). Jesus had female siblings (Mark 6:3). He also had male siblings named James, Joses, Judas, and Simon (Mark 6:3). He had lived in Nazareth, Galilee (Mark 1:9) and was baptized in the Jordan River (Mark 1:9) by a preacher named John (Mark 1:9), likely in the region of Judea (Mark 1:5).

Initially Jesus was probably a disciple of John, and it seems likely that some of John's disciples later became followers of Jesus. At a point in time, in Galilee Jesus began to proclaim an independent message of God's good news (Mark 1:14). It is not certain if his ministry began after John's arrest (Mark 1:14) which eventuated in John's beheading by Herod Antipas (Mark 6:27). It appears that Jesus remembered John with honor in his teachings (Matthew 11:7–8).

Jesus and his followers/companions would walk through the countryside and villages, and he would teach (Mark 6:6). Many were probably amazed that someone lacking formal education could be so articulate (John 7:15). Large groups of people likely gathered to hear him at various places, including the lake shore (Mark 2:13). He spent a considerable amount of time around Capernaum (Mark 1:21).

Jesus' behavior challenged purity practices. For example, he made a practice of eating with folks who were outcasts by the social and religious standards of the time (Mark 2:15) and perhaps even invited them to join in his travels (Mark 2:14). He was also likely to be flexible about Sabbath observances (Mark 2:23–28) and about dietary habits (Mark 7:15).

Without debating the method, we can confidently say, "Jesus cured some sick people." He likely cured a fever (Mark 1:30–31), a skin disorder (Mark 1:40–42), and a case of paralysis (Mark 2:12). On another occasion a woman's chronic vaginal flow stopped probably just by her trust in touching Jesus' garment (Mark 5:25–29), and there was likely more than one cure of a blind person (Mark 8:22–23; 10:46–52).

Further, Jesus had success in releasing people from demon possession (Luke 11:19–20), so much so that various religious authorities likely concluded that the power to do so must come from the chief demon Beelzebul (Mark 3:22); perhaps his biological family even thought that he was wasn't in his right mind (Mark 3:21). Jesus likely thought of his family in the broad sense of those who do the will of God (Thom 99:2). He probably refused to be tempted by calls for heavenly signs of God's kingdom/empire, whether demanded by Pharisees or by an anonymous voice in a crowd (cf. Mark 8:11–12).

Jesus likely made what turned out to be a final trip to Jerusalem (Mark 11:15). He probably created a disruptive incident in the Temple (Mark 11:15) where he also taught somewhat ambiguously about the comparative authority of Emperor and God (Mark 12:13). He was arrested (Mark 14:46), and his followers deserted him (Mark 14:50). The High Priest Caiaphas and the Roman governor Pilate probably took a personal interest in his fate (Mark 14:53; Mark 15:1). He was flogged (Mark 15:15) and crucified (Mark 15:24) by soldiers; probably a few stood a faithful watch, some women from among his followers, and they were at a safe distance (Mark 15:40–41).

After Jesus' death, within the time frame of a couple days to several years, probably Peter (1 Corinthians 15:5), but more certainly Mary Magdalene (John 20:11–18) and Paul (1 Corinthians 15:8), reported that Jesus "became visible" to them.

Reader Response Notes:

Reader Response Notes:

ATTITUDE ONE: MAKE YOUR LIFE COUNT

Facet One: Choose to live under divine authority.

1. Revere divine authority as Father.

"Father, hallowed (Scholars' Version:* "revered") be your name." (Luke 11:2; also Matthew 6:9)
    *Hereafter referenced as SV.

    Observation. Female divinities were worshipped across the ancient world. But in the ancient Jewish-Christian tradition the closest we come to that practice is perhaps most clearly expressed in the book of Proverbs, chapters 1–9, especially 8:22–36: "The Lord created me at the beginning of his work, the first of his acts of long ago. Ages ago I was set up (. . .) before the beginning of the earth (. . .) I was beside him like a master worker; and I was daily his delight (. . .)." The "me" and "I" in this passage refer to the Greek* word *Sophia* which is a feminine noun translated as "Wisdom." Compare John 1:1–14 where *Logos*, translated as "Word," is similarly described, but the gender of this noun is masculine.
    *The scripture manuscripts used by Jesus' followers were written in Greek.

2. The Father oversees nature with impartial care.

"He (the Father) makes his sun rise on the evil (SV: "bad") and on the good, and sends rain on the righteous (SV: "just") and on the unrighteous (SV: "unjust")." (Matthew 5:45)

3. We long to see the fulness of the Father's rule among us.

"Your kingdom (SV: "Empire")* come (SV: "be established")." (Luke 11:2; also Matthew 6:10)
    *Hereafter, wherever the NRSV uses "kingdom," assume that the SV uses "empire."

"It won't come by looking for it. They won't say, 'Look over here!' or 'Look over there!' Rather, The Father's kingdom is already spread out over the earth, and people don't see it." (Thomas 113:2-4)

"The kingdom of God is among you." (Luke17:21)

Facet Two: Be watchful for fundamental changes.

1. Something new is happening.

"New wine isn't put in old wineskins, because they'd (SV: "they might") burst. Nor is old wine put in new wineskins, because it'd (SV: "it might") spoil." (Thomas 47:4; also Luke 5:37-38; Mark 2:22; perhaps Matthew 9:17)

2. Something powerful is happening.

"I've cast fire on the world, and look, I'm watching over (SV: "guarding") it until it blazes." (Thomas 10; perhaps Luke 12:49)

3. Darkness is giving way to light.

"A city built on a hill (SV: "sitting on top of a mountain") cannot be hid." (Matthew 5:14; also Thomas 32)

"No one after lighting a lamp hides it under a jar (SV: "covers it with a pot"), or puts it under a bed but puts it on a lampstand, so that those who enter may see the light." (Luke 8:16; 11:33; also Mark 4:21; Matthew 5:15; Thomas 33:2-3)

"(. . .) nothing is hidden that won't be revealed." (Thomas 5:2; also Thomas 6:5; Luke 12:2; Matthew 10:26; Luke 8:17; Thomas 6:6)

4. There's no need for preoccupation with death.

"Become passersby." (Thomas 42)

Explanation. The phrase "passersby" was "common in ancient grave epitaphs." As a criticism of preoccupation with graves, "the point would be to keep on walking."[12]

"(. . .) let the dead bury their own dead."[13] (Matthew 8:22; also Luke 9:59–60)

Explanation. This saying probably refers to second burial practices; for example, reburial in ossuaries. The meaning would be: "Let the dead (in the tombs) re-bury their own dead."

5. Let's celebrate.

"The wedding guests (SV: "groom's friends") cannot fast while the bridegroom (SV: "groom," also below) is with them, can they? As long as they have the bridegroom with them, they cannot fast." (Mark 2:19; also Matthew 9:15; Luke 5:34; perhaps Thomas 104:2–3)

Facet Three: The demonic world is teetering.

Clarification. This section is not to be construed as an argument for the contemporary existence of a spirit world where demons are fighting a deity for control of human life. These references are, however, part of a first century belief system which included demons.

1. Demons are being exorcised.

Event. "Jesus drove out what were thought to be demons."[14]

"But no one can enter a strong man's house and plunder his property without first tying up the strong man; then indeed the house can be plundered." (Mark 3:27; also Matthew 12:29; Thomas 35:1–2; Luke 11:21–22)

"Every kingdom divided against itself becomes a desert (SV: "is devastated"), and house falls on house (SV: "a house divided against itself falls"). If Satan also is divided against himself, how will his kingdom stand (SV: "endure")? – for you say that I cast out the demons by Beelzebul." (Luke 11:17–18; also Matthew 12:25–26; perhaps Mark 3:23–26)

"Now if I cast (SV: "drive", here and twice below) out demons by Beelzebul, by whom do your exorcists cast them out? Therefore, they will be your judges. But if it is by the finger of God that I cast out the demons, then the kingdom of God has come to you." (Luke 11:19–20; perhaps Matthew 12:27–28)

2. Satan is in a free-fall.

"I watched Satan fall from heaven like a flash of lightning." (Luke 10:18)

Facet Four: Take your life in a different direction.

1. Trust that you will find life by losing your life.

"Those who try to make their life secure (SV: "hang on to their life") will lose it, but those who lose their life will keep (SV: "preserve") it." (Luke 17:33; cf. Matthew 16:25, 10:39; Luke 9:24; John 12:25; Mark 8:35)

"For whoever does the will of my Father in heaven is my brother and sister and mother." (Matthew 12:50; also Thomas 99:2; Luke 8:21; compare Mark 3:33–35; Thomas 99:3)

Rephrasing. God as Jesus' personal Father appears to be a special status given by Matthew's sector of the early church. So I prefer the reading in Mark and Luke, where all family members, including Jesus, have the same status doing God's will: "Whoever does God's will, that's my brother and sister and mother" (Mark 3:35). "My mother and my brothers are those who (SV: "listen to God's message") hear the word of God and do it. (Luke 8:21)

"Foxes have holes (SV: "dens"), and birds of the air (SV: "sky") have nests, but the Son of Man (SV: "Human One") has nowhere to lay (SV: "rest") his head." (Luke 9:58; also Matthew 8:20; Thomas 86:1–2)

Explanation. I know of no instance where the writers of the Jesus story indicate that he is without lodging; therefore, I understand this "foxes have dens" statement to be a metaphor for one who loses life; "it's like" having no place to stay. Thomas, in fact, intends 'son of man' to be understood in terms of "the Semitic idiom meaning simply 'human being'."[15]

Observation. In this teaching Jesus references himself as "Son of Man" (Greek: *uios tou anthropou*); more likely the title was bestowed on Jesus by the early church. The title is likely based on Jewish tradition (Daniel 7:13-14) where a mythical/heavenly "one like a son of man coming with the clouds of heaven" is served by all nations and peoples; compare, for example, the language describing the expected coming of the risen Jesus at Mark 13:26-27, Matthew 24:30-31, and Luke 21:27.

2. Save your life from Caesar. Speak truth to power.

"Give to Caesar what belongs to Caesar, give to God what belongs to God, (Thomas 100:2; also Mark 12:17; Luke 20:25; Matthew 22:21)

Explanation. The irony of the emperor and God comparison is that, no matter who the ruler may be, everything belongs to God.

Observation. The phrase "speaking truth to power" seems to be associated with post World War 2 Quaker traditions. A search of the internet quickly reveals a number of inspiring books with the phrase used in the titles.

Facet Five: Be attuned to those who are willing to lose life.

"A sower went out to sow (. . .) seed fell on the path (. . .) other seed fell on rocky ground (. . .) other seed fell among thorns (. . .) so they yielded no grain. Other seed fell into good soil and brought forth grain, growing up and increasing and yielding thirty and sixty and a hundredfold." (Mark 4:3–8; also Matthew 13:3–8; Thomas 9:1–5; Luke 8:5–8)

"Whoever has something-in-hand will be given more, but whoever doesn't have anything will lose even what little they do have." (Thomas 41:1–2; also Mark 4:25; Luke 8:18; cf. Matthew 25:29, 13:1; Luke 19:26)

"Strive (SV: "Struggle") to enter through the narrow door; for many, I tell you, will try to enter and will not be able." (Luke 13:24; cf. Matthew 7:13–14)

Interpretation. Pursue a willingness to lose life (the narrow door), find losing-life (something-in-hand), find others willing to lose life (the fertile soil), and share Jesus' attitudes (sow seeds).

Reader Response Notes:

Reader Response Notes:

ATTITUDE TWO: PRACTICE GOAL-ORIENTED PASSION

Hypothesis. Why would Jesus, whose over-arching attitude is other-centered, e.g., encouragement to love enemies, provide this rather substantial body of work seeming to largely advocate passionate pursuit of self-centered goals? First, I'm thinking that Jesus put humankind's range of self-centered behavior into the service of other-centeredness, saying, so to speak, "Certainly you can put this much effort into pursuing God's way/kingdom." Second, I suggest that Jesus used the stories to clarify his own behavior, to illustrate his passion for his own goals.

Facet One: Be an admirer of John the Baptist.

1. Imitate the sense of urgency in the Baptist's coming-judge language.

Preaching event. "In those days, John the Baptizer appeared in the wilderness of Judea, proclaiming, ... 'Even now the axe is lying at the root of the trees. Every tree therefore that does not bear good fruit is cut down and thrown into the fire (. . .) one who is more powerful than I is coming after me... His winnowing fork is in his hand, and he'll clear his threshing floor, and will gather his wheat into the granary, but the chaff he will burn with unquenchable fire.'" (Matthew 3:1, 10–12; also Luke 3:9, 17, 21)

2. Identify with John's strength as a man of the people.

"What did you (crowds) go out into the wilderness to look (SV: "gawk") at? A reed shaken by the wind? What then did you go out to see? Someone dressed in soft robes (SV: "Fancy clothes," also below)? Look, those who wear soft robes are in royal palaces (SV: "regal quarters")." (Matthew 11:7–8; also Thomas 78:1-2; Luke 7:24–25)

Baptism Event. "In those days Jesus came from Nazareth of Galilee and was baptized by John in the Jordan." (Mark 1:9; also Matthew 3: 13–17; Luke 3:21)

Hypothesis. For an unknown length of time Jesus was a disciple of John the Baptist.[16]

Facet Two: Match the passion of those who have some other-centered motives.

1. Equal the persistence of the vine-keeper.

"A man had a fig tree planted in his vineyard; and he came looking for fruit on it and found none. So he said to the gardener (SV: "vine-keeper"), 'See here! For three years I have come looking for fruit on this fig tree, and still I find none. Cut it down! Why should it be wasting (SV: "suck the nutrients out of the") soil?' He replied, 'Sir, let it stand alone for one more year, until I dig around it and put manure on it. If it bears fruit next year, well and good; but if not, you (SV: "we") can cut it down.'" (Luke 13:6–9)

Observation. In spite of several years of frustration the vine-keeper does all he can with the goal of success in mind, pursuing the goal even when the matter seems hopeless. In Mark 11 the failure of the fig tree to produce fruit is a symbol for the failure of the temple, but might we say that the fourth year had come and gone, and in Jesus' mind the time had come to take "cut it down" action.

2. Equal the intensity of the badgering friend.

"Suppose one of you has a friend, and you go to him at midnight and say to him,* 'Friend, lend me three loaves of bread, for a friend of mine has arrived, and I have nothing to set before him.' And he answers from within, 'Do not bother me; the door has already been locked, and my children are with me in bed. I can not get up and give you anything.' I tell you, even though he will not get up and give him anything because

he is his friend, at least because of his persistence (SV: "shameless behavior") he will get up and give him whatever he needs." (Luke 11:5–8)
*The narrator plays the reluctant friend role in the SV.

Observation. The center of the story is the strong level of persistence which leads to the hero's success, outlasting one who seems equally counter-motivated; social expectation demands something from him, and he vigorously pursues the obligation.

3. Equal the risk level of the shepherd's search.

"Which one of you having a hundred sheep and losing one of them, does not leave the ninety-nine in the wilderness and go after the one that is lost until he finds it? When he has found it, he lays it on his shoulders and rejoices. And when he comes home, he calls together his friends and neighbors, saying to them, 'Rejoice with me, for I have found my sheep that was lost.'" (Luke 15:4–6; also Matthew 18:12–13; Thomas 107:1–3)

Observation. A shepherd is rewarded with community celebration after putting his livelihood at risk in pursuit of ensuring the safety of one sheep.

Facet Three: Match the passion of those whose motives are primarily self-centered.

1. Equal the persistence of the home manager.

"What woman having ten silver coins* (SV: "ten drachmas"), if she loses one of them, does not light a lamp, sweep the house, and search carefully (SV: "high and low") until she finds it? When she has found it, she calls together her friends and neighbors, saying, 'Rejoice with me, for I have found the coin that I had lost.'" (Luke 15:8–9)
*A drachma equals about a day's wage for a laborer."[17]

Observation. The tireless effort of a woman is celebrated by neighbors who could no doubt identify with her circumstances.

2. Equal the level of sacrifice of the merchant.

"The kingdom of Heaven is like a merchant in search of fine pearls; on finding one pearl of great value (SV: "one priceless pearl") , he went out and sold all that he had and bought it." (Matthew 13:45–46; also Thomas 76:1–2)

Observation. The lesson is in the huge self-sacrifice required for the worthy result.

3. Equal the intensity of the self-castrator.

"There are eunuchs (SV: "castrated Men," here and below) who have been so since birth, and there are eunuchs who have been made eunuchs by others, and there are eunuchs who have made themselves eunuchs for the sake of the kingdom of heaven." (Matthew 19:12)

Observation. Even neutering oneself is not too outlandish an example of passionate goal pursuit for the highest possible goal.

Facet Four: Match the passion of those who are morally and/or legally compromised.

1. Equal the self-saving desperation of the manager.

"There was a rich man who had a manager, and charges were brought to him that this man was squandering his property. So he summoned him and said to him, 'What is this that I hear about you? Give me an account of your management (SV: "turn in your record books"), because you can't be my manager any longer.' Then the manager said to himself, 'What will I do now that my master is taking the position away from (SV: "firing") me? I am not strong enough to dig, and I am ashamed to beg (. . .) I have decided what do so that (. . .) people may welcome me into their homes (SV: "doors will open for me").' So summoning his master's debtors one by one, he asked the first, 'How much do you owe my master?' (. . .) '100 jugs (SV: "500 gallons") of olive oil.' He said (. . .) 'make it 50' (SV: "250"). Then he asked another, 'How much do you owe?' He replied, 'A thousand containers (SV: "bushels") of wheat.' He says to him (. . .) 'make it 800.' And his master commended the dishonest manager because he had acted shrewdly (SV: "prudently);'" (Luke 16:1–8)

Interpretation. At the end of the story the author seems to be using the word "shrewdly" in the popular colloquial sense of "hedged his bets." The dictionary definitions for the underlying Greek term *phronimos* are: sensible, thoughtful, prudent, wise.

Observation: A person, already a criminal, is admired for additional law-breaking behavior in desperate pursuit of self-preservation.

2. Equal the deceptive intensity of the treasure-hunter.

"The kingdom of Heaven is like treasure hidden in a field, which someone found and hid (SV: "covered up again"); then in his joy he goes and sells all that he has and buys that field. (Matthew 13:44)

Observation. This is a story of personal gain based on cheating someone out of a treasure that is legally theirs. The hero loses all self-respect and all possessions, but he couldn't be happier. Do whatever it takes to get what you want and then experience the joy.

3. Equal the widow's self-serving harassment.

"In a certain city (SV: "town," also below) there was a judge who neither feared God nor had respect for people. In that city there was a widow who kept coming to him and saying, 'Grant me justice (SV: "a ruling") against my opponent.' For a while he refused; but later he said to himself, 'Though I have no fear of God and no respect for anyone, yet because this widow keeps bothering me I will grant her justice (SV:

"rule in her favor"), so that she may not wear me out by continually coming.'" (Luke 18:2–5)

Interpretation. Here is a judge who doesn't allow his decisions to be influenced by God or humans. He meets his match in a woman whose unethical tenacity is stronger than all contrary forces. The phrase "wear me out," Greek *upopiazo*, has a dictionary definition of "strikes me under the eye." This phrase moves the reader from an abstract to a visceral understanding of the story. The woman is determined beyond all reasonableness to get her way.

Observation. This story places us in the bind of supporting the historical ideal of the widow as heroine in spite of behavior which undermines the justice system by using privilege to pursue selfish gain. Widows were especially cared for by God in Jewish tradition: see Psalms 146:9; James 1:27; Acts 6:1–6,

4. Equal the murderous intensity of an assassin.

"The Father's kingdom can be compared to a man who wanted to kill someone powerful. He drew his sword in his house and drove it into the wall to figure out whether his hand was strong enough. Then he killed the powerful one." (Thomas 98:1–3)

Observation. Here we have a reflection on political assassination to illustrate the outrageous single-mindedness required for pursuing God's way.

5. Equal the farmers' murderous desire for land.

"A [creditor] (SV: "greedy man") owned a vineyard. He leased it out to some sharecroppers (SV: "farmers," also below) to work it so he could collect its fruit. He sent his servant (SV: "slave," also below) so that the sharecroppers could give him the fruit of the vineyard. They seized his servant, beat him, and nearly killed him. The servant went back and told his master. His master said, 'Maybe he just didn't know them.' He sent another servant, but the tenants (SV: "farmers") beat that one too. Then the master sent his son, thinking, 'Maybe they'll show some respect to my son.' Because they knew that he was the heir of the vineyard, the sharecroppers seized and killed him." (Thomas 65:1–7; compare Mark 12:1–8; Matthew 21:33–39; Luke 20:9–15)

Explanation. Here again Jesus uses the theme of murder to make his point about goal-oriented passion. The tenants were willing to sacrifice their humanity, so to speak, to get possession of the vineyard.

Reader Response Notes:

Reader Response Notes:

ATTITUDE THREE: BE OTHER-CENTERED IN RELATIONSHIPS

Facet One: Predict motivation by means of outward behavior.

"There is nothing outside a person that by going in can defile, but the things that come out are what defile." (Mark 7:15; also Thomas 14:5; Matthew 15:10–11)

"Why do you wash the outside of the cup? Don't you know that whoever created (SV: "made," also below) the inside created the outside too?" (Thomas 89:1–2; compare Matthew 23:25–26; Luke 11:39–41)

Interpretation. Outward behavior is one and the same with inner conditions. This conclusion is based on Miller's observation of Mark 7:4 where we find the word *baptizo* (to immerse) used to describe the washing of cups and pots. There's no way to avoid cleaning both the outside and inside together.[18]

"Are grapes gathered from thorns or figs from thistles?" (Matthew 7:16; also Thomas 45:1; Luke 6:44)

Facet Two: Choose not to judge others.

1. Judge yourself, first and foremost.

"You see the speck (SV: "sliver," also below) that's in your brother's* (SV: "friend's," also below) eye, but you don't see the beam (SV: "timber," also below) in your own eye. When you get the beam out of your own eye, then you'll be able to see clearly to get the speck out of your brother's eye." (Thom 26:1–2; also Matthew 7:3–5, Luke 6:41–42)
   *Matthew and Luke use the term "neighbor."

"Two men went up to the temple to pray (. . .) The Pharisee, standing by himself, was praying (SV: "prayed silently") thus, 'God, I thank you that I am not like other people, thieves, rogues (SV: "unjust"), adulterers, or even like this tax (SV: "toll," also below) collector. I fast twice a week; I give a tenth of all my income.' But the tax collector standing far off would not even look up to heaven, but was beating his breast and saying, 'God, be merciful to me, a sinner. (Luke 18:10–13)

2. Be healers of society's outcasts, not their judges.

Event. "And as he sat at dinner (. . .) many tax (SV: "toll," also below") collectors and sinners were also sitting with Jesus and his disciples (. . .) When the scribes (SV: "scholars") of the Pharisees saw him (. . .) they said to his disciples (. . .) 'Why does he eat with tax collectors and sinners?'" (Mark 2:15-16, Matthew 9:10-11, Luke 5:29-30, Gospel Fragment 1224 5:1-2)

Explanation. Tax (toll) collectors were employees of businessmen in subjected territories contracted by Roman authorities to raise revenues. The Pharisees considered their actions to be equivalent to sinners, those who did not observe the laws of the God of the Jews.[19] Such offenses ranged from work activities on the Sabbath to prostitution.

"Those who are well have no need of a physician, but those who are sick." (Mark 2:17; also Matthew 9:12, Luke 5:31)

3. Be motivated by nonjudgmental compassion.

"A man was going down from Jerusalem to Jericho and fell into the hands of robbers, who stripped him, beat him, and went away, leaving him half dead (. . .) a priest was going down that road (. . .) he passed by on the other side (. . .) a Levite,* when he came to the same place and saw him, passed by on the other side. But a Samaritan (. . .) was moved with pity. He went to him and bandaged his wounds (. . .) Then he put him on to his own animal, brought him to an inn, and took care

of him. The next day he took out two denarii,** gave them to the innkeeper, and said, 'Take care of him; and when I come back, I will repay you whatever more you spend.'" (Luke 10:30 –35)
   *A Levite was a layman assigned religious duties in the temple.
   **A denarius was worth a day's wage for a laborer.[20]

Explanation. Priests and Levites conducted the affairs of the Temple in Jerusalem. By the legal traditions of the temple they were motivated to keep themselves ritually clean. That would include the avoidance of dead bodies, which was probably the appearance of this traveler.[21]

Explanation. The Samaritans were "(. . .) descended from the Israelites who had remained behind when the Assyrians deported the leading families of the region following their conquest in 722 B.C.E. (. . .)." They intermarried with foreigners, built their own temple when there was none yet in Jerusalem, followed the same law books as those who were originally exiled, and settled in Judea. The first century historian Josephus reports a murderous conflict between the two groups (52 C.E.), requiring Roman intervention.[22]

Observation. Subject of longstanding historical animosity with Judeans, a Samaritan turns out to be the non-judgmental healer.

4. Be aware that God's way does not use society's standards to classify people.

"The kingdom of heaven is like a landowner who went out early in the morning to hire laborers for his vineyard. After agreeing with the laborers for the usual daily wage (SV: "a denarius," also below), he sent them into his vineyard (. . .) When he went out about nine o'clock (. . .) noon (. . .) three o'clock (. . .) and five o'clock (. . .) he found others standing around in the market place, and said, 'You also go into the vineyard, as well, and I will pay you whatever is right.' (. . .) When those hired about five o'clock came, each of them received the usual daily wage. Now when the first came (. . .) each of them also received the usual daily wage. And when they received it, they grumbled against the landowner. '(…) You have made them equal to us who have borne the burden of the day and the scorching heat.' (. . .) But he replied to one of them, 'Friend (. . .), I choose to give to this last the same as I give you (. . .) with what belongs to me (. . .).'" (Matthew 20:1–15)

"There was a man who had two sons. The younger of them said (. . .) 'Father, give me the share of the property that will belong to me.' So he divided his property between them (. . .) the younger son gathered all that he had and traveled to a distant country where he squandered his property in dissolute living (. . .) a severe famine took place throughout that country (. . .) He would have gladly filled himself with the pods that the pigs were eating; (. . .) 'I will get up and go to my father, and I will say to him (. . .) I am no longer worthy to be called your son; treat me like one of your hired hands'(. . .) while he still was far off, his father saw him and was filled with compassion (. . .) the father said to his slaves (. . .) 'Quickly, bring out a robe (. . .) a ring (. . .) sandals (. . .) let us eat and celebrate; for this son of mine was dead and is alive again.'(. . .) Now his elder son was in the field; and when he came and approached the house, he heard music and dancing. He called one of the slaves (SV: "servant boys") and asked what was going on (. . .) He replied, 'Your brother has come home' (. . .) Then he became angry and refused to go in (. . .) His father came out and began to plead with him. But he answered his father, 'Listen! For all these years I have been working like a slave for you, and I have never disobeyed your command; yet you have never given me even a young goat so that I might celebrate with my friends. But when this son of yours came back who has devoured your property with prostitutes, you kill the fatted calf for him.' Then the father said to him, 'Son you are always with me, and all that is mine is yours. But we had to celebrate and rejoice because this brother of yours (. . .) was lost and has been found.'" (Luke 15:11–32)

Facet Three: Choose to reject vengeful motives.

1. Use love to imitate Nature's impartiality toward good and evil.

"For he (your Father*) makes his sun rise on the evil (SV: "bad") and on the good, and sends rain on the righteous (SV: "just) and on the unrighteous (SV: "unjust)." (Matthew 5:45)
  *Earlier in the passage God is referred to as Father.

"Love your enemies (. . .)." (Luke 6:27; also Matthew 5:44)

"If you love those who love you, what merit is there in that? After all, even sinners love those who love them (. . .) But love your enemies (. . .)." (Luke 6:32, 35; also Matthew 5:46)

2. Be generous when unfairly burdened.

"If anyone strikes (SV: "slaps") you on the right cheek, turn the other also;" (Matthew 5:39b; Luke 6:29a)

"If anyone wants to sue you and take your coat (SV: "shirt"), give your cloak (SV: "coat") as well;" (Matthew 5:40; Luke 6:29b)

"And if anyone forces (SV: "conscripts") you to go one mile, go also the second mile." (Matthew 5:41)

3. See the capacity for good-will in an individual adversary.

"When you go (SV: "you're about to appear") with your accuser before a magistrate, on the way make an effort to settle the case, or you may be dragged before the judge, and the judge hand you over to the officer (SV: "jailer," twice), and the officer throw you in prison. I tell you, you will never get out until you have paid the very last penny." (Luke 12:58–59; also Matthew 5:25–26)

Facet Four: Choose to forgive others.

1. Forgive and you will receive forgiveness in return.

"Forgive us our debts as we also have forgiven our debtors." (Matthew 6:12)

"Forgive and you'll be forgiven;" (Luke 6:37)

2. Compromised forgiveness has no good outcome.

"(. . .) the kingdom of Heaven may be compared to a king (SV: "human ruler") who wished to settle accounts with his slaves (. . .) one who owed him ten thousand talents was brought to him; and, as he could not pay, his lord (SV: "ruler") ordered him to be sold (including family and possessions) and payment to be made. So the slave fell on his knees before him, saying, 'Be patient with me and I will pay you everything.' And out of pity for him, the lord (SV: "master," also three times below) of that slave released him and forgave the debt. But that same slave, as he went out, came upon one of his fellow slaves who owed him a hundred denarii; and seizing him by the throat, he said, 'Pay what you owe.' Then his fellow slave fell down and begged him, 'Have patience with me and I will pay you.' But he refused (. . .) and threw him into prison. (. . .) His fellow slaves (. . .) reported to their lord all that had taken place. (. . .) Then his lord summoned him, 'You wicked slave! I forgave you (. . .) Should you not have had mercy?' (. . .) And in anger the lord handed him over to be tortured until he would pay his entire debt." (Matthew 18:23–34)

Interpretation. One source estimates that the difference between 10000 talents and 100 denarii is the same as the difference between ten million dollars and ten dollars.[23] That difference gives the narrative an enormously exaggerated burlesque quality.

Interpretation. Facet Three presents Jesus as supporting forgiveness because it equalizes relationships and receives God's approval. The forgiveness received is equal to the amount given. But "forgiveness cannot be compromised without undesirable consequences."[24]

Reader Response Notes:

Reader Response Notes:

ATTITUDE FOUR: ENCOURAGE THE POWERLESS

Facet One: Speak Words of Hope to the Destitute.

"The last will be first, and the first will be last" (Matthew 20:16; also Mark 10:31; Matthew 19:30; compare Luke 13:30; Thomas 4:2)

"Blessed are (SV: "Congratulations") you who are poor, for yours is the kingdom of God." (Luke 6:20; also Thomas 54; compare Matthew 5:3).

"Blessed are (SV: "Congratulations") you who are hungry now, for you will be filled (SV: "have a feast")." (Luke 6:21; also Thom 69:2; compare Matthew 5:6)

"Blessed are (SV: "Congratulations") you who weep now, for you will laugh." (Luke 6:21; also Matthew 5:4)

Interpretation. The word "poor" seems not to be a strong enough translation for the underlying Greek term *ptochus*. Referencing Aristophanes' play *Plutus* (535-554), Crossan writes, "The Greek word *penes* means 'poor' and *ptochos* means 'destitute.' The former describes the status of a peasant family making a bare subsistence living...the latter indicates the status of a family pushed, by disease or debt, draught or death, off the land and into destitution and begging."[25]

Facet Two: Challenge oppressive social systems.

1. Challenge barriers to adult equality.

"If anyone strikes (SV: "slaps") you on the right cheek, turn the other also." (Matthew 5:39; also Luke 6:29)

Interpretation. A blow to the right cheek would require a left-handed humiliating slap, the left hand normally being used for toileting and other unclean activity in a society that valued purity. In the monastic-like Qumran community, for example, a left-hand gesture could result in being banned for a period of time. Jesus' words can be interpreted as demanding to be treated as an equal, i.e., to be given right-hand equality.[26]

2. Challenge the cruel and dismissive treatment of children.

"Let the little children (SV: "children") come to me; do not stop them; for it is to such as these that the kingdom of God belongs." (Mark 10:14; also Matthew 19:14; Luke 18:16; compare Thomas 22)

Interpretation. Crossan points out that there are no sexual distinctions or boundaries, and acceptance is unconditional in this material. For contrast he cites a letter of 1 B.C.E. (Oxyrhynchus Papyri 4.744) from Hilarion in Alexandria to his pregnant wife Alis in Oxyrhynchus, as evidence of the status of children in the "ancient Mediterranean" region: "If by chance you bear a son, if it is a boy, let it be; if it is a girl, cast it out (to die)." Crossan comments, "An infant was quite literally a nobody unless its father accepted it as a member of the family (. . .)" The context in which the authentic Jesus material is found – Jesus wants to touch, hold, and bless, and the disciples want to prevent contact – suggests that a dispute arose in the early church over what to do about abandoned infants. In some ways the tragedy was glossed over: Matthew 18:14 equates infancy with humility, Thomas 22 connects it to sexual asceticism, and John 3:1–10 ascribes it to recent baptism.[27]

Interpretation. "The Greek terms *pais* and *paidion*, usually translated 'child,' can mean slave or young slave, and can include boys, girls, and young men as witnessed to by contemporary papyri and the writings of Josephus and Philo. Would not the reign of God belong especially to child-slaves? The statement that young slaves were of God's kingdom would have been met with surprise or even shock by his hearers, especially the free, even if they were poor. Any who had been forced to see children into servitude, however, would have appreciated Jesus' subversive speech."[28]

3. Challenge demeaning loan requirements.

"From anyone who takes away your coat, do not withhold even your shirt." (Luke 6:29; also Matthew 5:40)

Interpretation. This puzzling directive could no doubt result in immediate laughter in a two-garment society. Jesus appears to be recalling Deuteronomy 24:10-14. To get a loan, as collateral the poor would lose their coat during the day. Here the debtor strips naked to shame this practice. The Manual of Discipline of the Qumran community is an example of advocating strict rules against exposing parts of the body.[29]

4. Challenge the practice of military conscription

"If anyone forces (SV: "conscripts") you to go one mile, go also the second mile." (Matthew 5:41)

Interpretation. Roman roads were marked by milestones. Soldiers were permitted to conscript natives to carry loads one mile. The offer to go a second mile would challenge this practice and shame this use of power.[30]

Facet Three: Practice the redistribution of income.

1. Give to those who live on the streets.

"Someone was planning on having guests. When dinner was ready, they (SV: "he") sent their (SV: "his") servant (SV: "slave," also six times hereafter) to call the visitors. The servant went to the first (. . .) They (SV: "who," three times hereafter) said, 'Some merchants owe me money. They're coming tonight. I need to go and give them instructions. Excuse me from the dinner.' The servant went to another (. . .) They said, 'I've just bought a house and am needed for the day. I won't have time.' The servant went to another (. . .) They said, 'My friend is getting married and I'm going to make dinner (SV: "arrange the banquet"). I can't come. Excuse me from the dinner.' The servant went to another one (. . .) They said, "I've just bought a farm (SV: "an estate") and am going to collect the rent. I can't come. Excuse me.' The servant went back and told the master, 'The ones you've invited to the dinner have excused themselves.' The master said to the servant, 'Go out to the roads and bring whomever you find so that they can have dinner.'" (Thomas 64:1–11; also Luke 14:16–23; compare Matthew 22:2–13).

2. Give without expectation of a return.

"Give to everyone who begs from you; (. . .)." (Matthew 5:42; cf. 6:30)

"If you have money, don't lend it at interest. Instead, give [it to] someone from whom you won't get it back." (Thomas 95:1–2; also Luke 6:35)

Interpretation. It would seem that "Lend-without-return is a global injunction that would lead to instant financial disaster (. . .). The requirement is absolute, it is devastating, and it therefore has a touch of humor."[31] As elsewhere, we are put into an interpretive quandary.

Reader Response Notes:

Reader Response Notes:

ATTITUDE FIVE: USE YOUR MONEY FOR UNSELFISH PURPOSES

Facet One: Oppose the individual harboring of wealth.

"It's easier for a camel to go (SV: "squeeze") through the eye of a needle than for someone who is rich to get into the kingdom of God." (Matthew 19:24: also Luke 18:25; Mark 10:25)

"There was a rich man who had much money. He said, 'I'll use (SV: "invest") my money to sow, reap, plant, and fill my barns (SV: "storehouses") with fruit (SV: "produce"), so that I won't need anything.' That's what he was thinking to himself (SV: "in his heart"), but he died that very night." (Thomas 63:1–6; also Luke 12:16–20)

"How hard it will be (SV: "is") for those who have wealth (SV: "with money") to enter God's empire." (Mark 10:23; also Luke 18:24; Matthew 19:23)

Facet Two: Reject money's interference with service to God.

"No slave can serve two masters; for a slave will either hate the one and love the other, or be devoted to the one and despise the other. You cannot serve (SV: "be enslaved to both") God and wealth (SV: "mammon")." (Luke 16:13: also Matthew 6:24; cf. Thomas 47:2)

Temple commercialization event. "Then they came to Jerusalem. And he entered the temple and began to drive out those (SV: "the vendors") who were selling and those (SV: "the customers") who were buying in the temple, (. . .)." (Mark 11:15; also Matthew 21:12; Luke 19:45; compare John 2:13-15)

Facet Three: Reject money's association with secular abuses of power and position.

"(. . .) a man going on a journey summoned his slaves and entrusted his property to them. To one he gave five talents, to another two, to another one, to each according to his ability. Then he went away. The one who had received the five talents went off at once and traded with them, and made five more talents. In the same way the one who had the two talents made two more talents. But the one who had received the one talent went out and dug a hole in the ground and hid his master's money. After a long time, the master of those slaves came and settled accounts with them. (. . .) His master said to the first, 'Well done, good and trustworthy slave. You have been trustworthy in a few things. so I will put you in charge of many things; enter into the joy of (SV: "come Celebrate with") your master.' (The master then commended the second slave with exactly the same words.) Then the one who had received the one talent also came forward, saying, 'Master I knew that you were a harsh (SV: "ruthless") man, reaping where you did not sow and gathering where you did not scatter seed; so I was afraid, and I went out and hid your talent in the ground. Here you have what is yours.' But his master replied, 'You wicked and lazy (SV: "incompetent and timid") slave! You knew, did you, that I reap where I did not sow and gather where I did not scatter? Then you ought to have invested my money with the bankers, and on my return I would have received what was my own with interest. So take the talent from him and give it to the one with ten talents. (Matthew 25:14–28; also Luke 19:13, 15–24)

Explanation. "These amounts are astronomical. One talent's worth of silver (a unit of weight, approximately 75 pounds), represents nearly twenty years' wages for a laborer."[32]

Interpretation. It's seems quite possible that the slave who buried the talent was courageous, refusing to participate in his master's ill-gotten gains, helping us to see that the parable is primarily urging just behavior and that it is not intended to be seen as a contrast in the motivation of the slaves.[33]

Facet Four: Practice the redistribution of income. See Attitude Four: Facet Three.

Facet Five: Don't be pretentious in giving.

"When you give alms (SV: "to charity"), do not let your left hand know what your right hand is doing."

Reader Response Notes:

Reader Response Notes:

ATTITUDE SIX: BE FLEXIBLE ABOUT THE USE OF TRADITION

Facet One: Do not trust the scribes/scholars.

"Beware of the scribes (SV: "scholars") who like to walk around in long robes, and love to be greeted with respect in the marketplaces, and to have the best (SV: "prominent") seats in the synagogues and places of honor (SV: "the best couches") at banquets." (Luke 20:46; also Mark 12:38–39; Matthew 23:5–7; Luke 11:43)

Observation. Of the 3% to 5% of the indigenous population in Roman occupied Palestine at the time of Jesus that could read and write, in the business world some would be scribes or clerks (Greek: *grammateus*) who could provide a receipt for a transaction such as a divorce or land acquisition. But scribe as used in Jesus' quote meant an elite group who held a special place in the eyes of the populace. They copied the Jewish scriptures and additionally read and commented on them, especially with regard to observance of the laws, at places of gathering.[34]

Facet Two: Re-think the kingdom/empire of God.[35]

1. The Kingdom/empire of God appreciates the inspiration of the past.

1a. *Torah Tradition.** To celebrate "the Lord's" visitation, "Abraham hastened into the tent to Sarah, and said, 'Make ready quickly three measures of choice flour, knead it, and make cakes' (. . .) Then one said, 'I will surely return to you in due season, and your wife Sarah shall have a son (. . .) Now Abraham and Sarah were old, advanced in age (. . .) so Sarah laughed to herself (. . .)." (Genesis 18:1–15)
 *Torah refers to the first five books of the Jewish Bible, a major division known as the Law.

"To what should I compare the kingdom of God? It is like yeast (SV: "leaven") that a woman took and mixed in with three measures (SV: "fifty pounds") of flour until all of it was leavened." (Luke 13:20–21; also Matthew 13:33; Thomas 96:1–2)

Observation. Jesus made positive use of details in the Torah when comparing God's kingdom/empire to a very large celebration of an anticipated miracle birth.

1b. *Torah Tradition.* "The Egyptians shall know that I am the Lord, when I stretch out my hand against Egypt and bring the Israelites out from among them (. . .) Then the Lord said to Moses, '(. . .) lift up your staff, and stretch out your hand over the sea and divide it, that the Israelites may go into the sea on dry ground (. . .)'" (Exodus 7:5; 14:15)

"Now if I cast out the demons by Beelzebul by whom do your exorcists cast them out? Therefore, they will be your judges. But if it is by the finger of God that I cast out the demons, then the kingdom of God has come to (SV: "for") you." (Luke 11:19–20; compare Matthew 12:27–28)

Observation. Jesus made positive use of a detail in the Torah (Moses' hand/staff = "finger") to help describe the availability of God's kingdom/empire.

1c. *Prophetic Tradition.** "Put in the sickle for the harvest is ripe (. . .) For the day of the Lord is near in the valley of decision." (Joel 3:13-14)
*The Prophets are also a major division of literature within the Jewish Bible. They are those commissioned by God to challenge those in power, most notably the people, priests, and kings of Israel and Judah (see Hosea 5:1).

"The kingdom of God is as if someone would scatter seed on the ground (. . .) the seed would sprout and grow, he does not know how (SV: "although the sower is unaware of it") (. . .) But when the grain is ripe, at once he goes in with his sickle, because the harvest has come." (Mark 4:26–29; compare Thom 21:9)

Observation. Jesus made positive use of the harvest vision of the prophet Joel to describe our anticipation of the kingdom/empire of God.

2. The kingdom/empire of God transforms evil.

Torah Tradition. "For seven days no leaven shall be found in your houses; for whoever eats what is leavened shall be cut off from the congregation of Israel." (Exodus 12:19)

"To what should I compare the kingdom of God? It is like yeast (SV: "leaven") that a woman took and mixed in with three measures (SV: "fifty pounds") of flour until all of it was leavened." (Luke 13:20–21; also Matthew 13:33; Thomas 96:1–2)

Observation. Jesus transforms a symbol (leaven) for being cut-off from the people of God into a symbol to indicate a celebratory connection with the people of God.

3. The power of God's kingdom/empire manifests itself in weakness.

Prophetic Tradition. "Thus says the Lord God, I myself will take a sprig from the lofty top of a cedar (. . .) I myself will plant it...on the mountain height of Israel (. . .) that it may become a noble cedar (. . .) in the shade of its branches will rest winged creatures of every kind. All the trees of the field shall know that I am the lord." (Ezekiel 17:22–24)

"(. . .) the kingdom of heaven (. . .) can be compared to a mustard seed. Though it's the smallest of all the seeds, when it falls on tilled soil it makes a plant so large (SV: "produces a large branch") that it shelters the birds of heaven (SV: "of the sky")." (Thomas 20:2-4: also Mark 4:30-32; Luke 13:18-19; Matthew 13:31-32)

Explanation. Jesus challenged, perhaps even mocked, the interpretation of God's kingdom/empire by the Prophet Ezekiel. The birds are to be protected by a mustard plant rather than a mighty Cedar tree. In the larger context of Ezekiel the birds are understood as the nations of the earth.

Facet Three: Use the Sabbath to Benefit Human Beings.

Torah Tradition. "Remember the Sabbath day and keep it holy. Six days you shall labor (. . .) But the seventh day (. . .) you shall not do any work. For in six days the Lord made heaven and earth (. . .) but rested the seventh day; therefore, the Lord blessed the Sabbath day and consecrated it." (Exodus 20:8–11; compare Deuteronomy 5:1–22; see also Genesis 1:26, *Psalms 4:4–8)
 *Here we have a response that also includes the poets and songsters (Psalms) of Jewish tradition.

"One sabbath* he was going through the grain fields; and as they made their way his disciples began to pluck (SV: "strip") heads of grain. The Pharisees said to him, 'Look, why are they doing what is not lawful (SV: "not permitted") on the sabbath?'" (Mark 2:23–24; compare Luke 6:1–2; Matthew 12:1)
 *Unlike the SV, sabbath is not capitalized in the NRSV.

"The sabbath was made for humankind, and not humankind for the sabbath.'" (Mark 2:27; compare Matthew 12:8; Luke 6:5)

Explanation. Certain religionists* among the Jews of Palestine held a strong influence over the populace and were devout about developing a list of rules for personal purity and piety before God. For example, specific rules defined how to rest from work on the Sabbath. Jesus apparently advocated a more flexible human friendly approach to sabbath behavior.
 *The gospels usually identify these religionists as Pharisees.

Facet Four: Trust God to care without first making demands. Also see Attitude Seven: Facet Two.

Historical Tradition.* "God answered Solomon, 'Because this was in your heart and you have not asked for possessions (. . .) or for the life of those who hate you (. . .) not even for long life, but have asked for wisdom and knowledge (. . .), wisdom and knowledge are granted to you. I will also give you riches, possessions, and honor, such as none of the kings had who were before you, and none after you shall have the like." (2 Chronicles 1:12)

*The History books, such as the Samuel, Kings, and Chronicles sagas, are another major division of the Jewish Bible.

"Consider the lilies, how they grow: They neither toil nor spin; yet I tell you, even Solomon in all his glory was not clothed like one of these. But if God so clothes the grass of the field, which is alive today and tomorrow is thrown into the oven, how much more will he clothe (SV: "take care of") you – you of little faith (SV: "meager trust")." (Luke 12:27–28: also Matthew 6:28–30; Thomas 36:2)

Explanation. We are given a list of things that Solomon did to earn his reward, but the lilies outshine him even though they did nothing to earn their beauty.

Reader Response Notes:

Reader Response Notes:

ATTITUDE SEVEN: REPLACE ANXIETY WITH TRUST

Facet One: Do not waste your energy on anxiety.

"And can any of you by worrying add a single hour to your span of life." (Luke 12:25; also Matthew 6:27)

"Don't be anxious from morning to evening or from evening to morning about what you'll wear." (Thomas 36:1; also Luke 12:22–23; Matthew 6:25)

"And why do you worry about clothing?" (Matthew 6:28)

Facet Two: Trust God to care without first making demands. See Attitude Six: Facet Four.

"Consider the lilies, how they grow: They neither toil nor spin; yet I tell you, even Solomon in all his glory was not clothed like one of these. But if God so clothes the grass of the field, which is alive today and tomorrow is thrown into the oven, how much more will he clothe (SV: "take care of") you – you of little faith (SV: "meager trust")." (Luke 12:27–28: also Matthew 6:28–30; Thomas 36:2)

"Consider the ravens: they neither sow nor reap, they have neither storehouse nor barn, and yet God feeds them. Of how much more value are you than the birds." (Luke 12:24; also Matthew 6:26)

"Are not five sparrows sold for two pennies?* Yet not one of them is forgotten (SV: "overlooked") in God's sight. But even the hairs of your head are all counted. Do not be afraid (SV: "timid"); you are of more value than many (SV: "a flock of") sparrows. (Luke 12:6–7; also Matthew 10:29–31)
    *SV 1993: "What do sparrows cost? A dime a dozen?" The cost is represented by the Greek word *assarion*, which has the dictionary definition of 1/16 of a denarius, or roughly one cent.

Facet Three: Expect basic needs to be met.

"Ask, and it will be given you; search, and you will find; knock, and the door will be opened for you. For every one who asks receives, and everyone who searches, finds, and for everyone who knocks, the door will be opened." (Matthew 7:7–8; also Luke 11:9–10; Thomas 94:1–2; 2:1)

1. Expect to be physically nourished.

"Is there anyone among you who, if your Child asks for bread, will give a stone? Or if the Child asks for fish will give him a snake? If you then, who are evil (SV: "worthless"), know how to give good gifts to your children, how much more will your Father in heaven give good things to those who ask him? (Matthew 7:9–11; also Luke 11:11–13)

"Our Father (. . .) Give us this day our daily bread." (Matthew 6:11; also Luke 11:3)

2. Expect to be healed.

Event. "(. . .) a blind beggar (. . .) began to shout out and say, 'Jesus, Son of David, have mercy on me!' Many sternly ordered him to be quiet (SV: "shut up"), but he cried out even more (. . .) 'Take heart, get up, he is calling you.' So throwing off his cloak, he sprang up and came to Jesus (. . .) 'My teacher (SV: "Rabbi"), let me see again.' (. . .) Immediately he regained his sight (. . .)." (Mark 10:46–52; Matthew 20:29–34; Luke 18:35–43)

Event. "Now there was a woman who had been suffering from hemorrhages for twelve years (. . .) She had heard about Jesus, and came up behind him in the crowd and touched his clothes (. . .) Immediately her hemorrhage stopped; and she felt in her body that she was healed of her disease (. . .)." (Mark 5:25–29; also Matthew 9:20–22; Luke 8:43–44)

Interpretation. "The kind of blindness Jesus was able to cure was subject to psychosomatic therapy: blindness that had an organic basis would have required magic for a cure, and Jesus was probably not a magician."[36] Other psychosomatic conditions would be susceptible to cures, as well.

3. Expect a generous supply.

"The kingdom of God is as if someone would scatter seed on the ground, (. . .) The seed would sprout and grow, he does not know how (SV: "although the sower is unaware of it"). The earth produces of itself (. . .) But when the grain is ripe, at once he goes in with his sickle, because the harvest has come." (Mark 4:26–29; compare Thomas 21:9)

"A sower went out to sow (. . .) some seed fell on the path (. . .) other seed fell on Rocky ground (. . .) other seed fell among thorns (. . .) and they yielded no grain. Other seed fell into good soil and brought forth grain, growing up and increasing and yielding thirty, sixty, and a hundredfold." (Mark 4:3–8; also Matthew 13: 3–8; Thomas 9:1–5; Luke 8:5-8)

Reader Response Notes:

Reader Response Notes:

ATTITUDE EIGHT: TAKE ON OUTREACH RESPONSIBILITY

Facet One: Accept the Hospitality Offered on the Road.

1. Accept Lodging.

"Remain in the same house, eating and drinking whatever they provide." (Luke 10:7)

2. Accept Meals.

"If they welcome you (SV: "people take you in") when you enter any land (SV: "region") and go around in the countryside, (..) eat whatever they give you (. . .)." (Thomas 14:4; also Luke 10:8)

Facet Two: Be prepared for discouragement.

1. Those who know you best will be your harshest judges.

"No prophet is welcome in their own village." (Thomas 31:1; also Luke 4:24, John 4:44, Matthew 13:57; Mark 6:4)

2. Some successes will turn to failure.

"Salt is good; but if salt has lost its saltiness (SV: "becomes tasteless"), how can you season (SV: "renew") it?" (Mark 9:50; also Luke 14:34–35; Matthew 5:13)

"When the unclean spirit has gone out of a person, it wanders through waterless regions looking for a resting a place, but not finding any it says, 'I will return to my house from which I came.' When it comes, it finds it swept and put in order. Then it goes and brings seven other spirits more evil than itself, and they enter and live there; and the last state of that person is worse than the first." (Luke 11:24–26; also Matthew 12:43–45)

3. People will resist change.

"No one after drinking old wine wants new wine." (Luke 5:39; also Thomas 47:3)

Facet Three: Hold firm when your coping skills are challenged.

"Be wise as serpents and innocent as doves." (SV: "You must be as sly as snakes and simple as pigeons.") (Matthew 10:16; also Thomas 39:3)

Facet Four: Stand fast to the demands for going to Jerusalem.

1. Release yourself from the priority of family authority.

"Whoever comes to me and does not hate father and mother, wife and children, brothers and sisters, yes, and even life itself (SV: "your own life"), cannot be my disciple." (Luke 14:26; compare Thomas 55:1–2; Matthew 10:37)

2. Create conditions from which kingdom behaviors can emerge unknown to you.

"The Father's kingdom can be compared to a woman carrying a jar of flour (SV: "meal"). While she was walking down [a] long road (SV: "along a distant road"), the jar's handle broke and the flour spilled out behind her on the road. She didn't know it, and didn't realize there was a problem until she got home, put down the jar, and found it empty." (Thomas 97:1-4)

Observation. Jackson advises that regarding "the mealie-meal (coarse maize flour) emptying from the jar (. . .) once an object is on the woman's head, she no longer feels its weight. Indeed, I have seen loads that take two strong men to lift onto a woman's head that she then carries with ease. And she would not have felt the mealie-meal draining out or trickling down her body because she undoubtedly had a baby wrapped on her back and was carrying water jars in each hand."[37]

Compare. "It won't come by looking for it. They won't say, 'Look over here!' or 'Look over there!' Rather, The Father's kingdom is already spread out over the earth, and people don't see it." (Thomas 113:2–4)

Compare. "When you give (SV: "to charity") alms, do not let your left hand know what your right hand is doing." (Matthew 6:3; also Thomas 62:2)

Reader Response Notes:

Reader Response Notes:

Looking Forward

Crossan reminds us that in ancient society there were really only two classes: a very small upper class and a very large lower class:

"Those without power could be clients to the patrons above them (. . .) Brokers were clients to those above them and patrons to those below (. . .) Patronage and clientage at their best gave some hope or chance to individuals among the lower classes, but at their worst they confirmed dependency, maintained hierarchy, sustained oppression, and stabilized domination (. . .)" On the other hand, Jesus stood for "the equal sharing (. . .) of miracle and table" living out "the kingdom of God (. . .) in which individuals are in direct contact with one another and with God, unmediated by any established brokers or fixed locations."[38]

Each of us is faced with the challenge of taking the attitudes of Jesus seriously. We, of course, do not live in the first century and do not have to face the challenge of trusting enough to make a literal decision, as did some followers, about going to Jerusalem with him. But each of us does have to trust enough to decide and follow through on this question: "What is crucial to me in the 21st century?" Does it look in any way like a society of equals?

Reader Response Notes:

Reader Response Notes:

Appendix One: Summary of Attitudes

Attitude One: Make your life count.

Facet One: Choose to live under divine authority.

1. Revere divine authority as Father.
2. The Father oversees nature with impartial care.
3. We long to see the fulness of the Father's rule among us.

Facet Two: Be watchful for fundamental changes.

1. Something new is happening.
2. Something powerful is happening.
3. Darkness is giving way to light.
4. There's no need for preoccupation with death.
5. Let's celebrate.

Facet Three: The demonic world is teetering.

1. Demons are being exorcised.
2. Satan is in a free fall.

Facet Four: Take your life in a different direction.

1. Trust that you will find life by losing your life.
2. Save your life from Caesar. Speak truth to power.

Facet Five: Be attuned to those who are willing to lose life.

Attitude Two: Practice goal-oriented passion.

Facet One: Be an admirer of John the Baptist.

1. Imitate the sense of urgency in the Baptist's apocalyptic coming-judge language.
2. Identify with John's strength as a man of the people.

Facet Two: Match the passion of those who have some other-centered motives.

1. Equal the persistence of the vine-keeper.
2. Equal the intensity of the badgering friend.
3. Equal the risk-level of the shepherd's search.

Facet Three: Match the passion of those whose motives are primarily self-entered.

1. Equal the persistence of the home manager.
2. Equal the level of sacrifice of the merchant.
3. Equal the intensity of the self-castrator.

Facet Four: Match the passion of those whose motives are morally and/or legally compromised.

1. Equal the self-saving desperation of the manager.
2. Equal the deceptive intensity of the treasure-hunter.
3. Equal the widow's self-serving harassment.
4. Equal the murderous intensity of an assassin.
5. Equal the farmers' murderous desire for land.

Attitude Three: Be other-centered in relationships.

Facet One: Predict motivation by means of outward behavior.

Facet Two: Choose not to judge others.

1. Judge yourself, first and foremost.

2. Be healers of society's outcasts, not their judges.
3. Be motivated by nonjudgmental compassion.
4. Be aware that God's way does not use society's standards to classify people.

Facet Three: Choose to reject vengeful motives.

1. Use love to Imitate nature's impartiality toward good and evil.
2. Be generous when unfairly burdened.
3. See the capacity for good-will in an individual adversary.

Facet Four: Choose to forgive others.

1. Forgive and you will receive forgiveness in return.
2. Compromised forgiveness has no good outcome.

Attitude Four: Encourage the powerless.

Facet One: Speak words of hope to the destitute.

Facet Two: Challenge oppressive social systems.

1. Challenge barriers to adult equality.
2. Challenge the cruel and dismissive treatment of children.
3. Challenge loan requirements.
4. Challenge the practice of military conscription.

Facet Three: Practice the redistribution of income.
(See Attitude Five: Facet Four.)

1. Give to those who live on the streets.
2. Give without expectation of return.

Attitude Five: Use your money for unselfish purposes.

Facet One: Oppose the individual harboring of wealth.

Facet Two: Reject money's interference with service to God.

Facet Three: Reject money's association with secular abuses of power and position.

Facet Four: Practice the redistribution of income.
(See Attitude Four: Facet Three.)

Facet Five: Do not be pretentious in giving.

Attitude Six: Be flexible in the use of tradition.

Facet One: Do not trust the scribes/scholars.

Facet Two: Rethink the kingdom/empire of God.

1. The kingdom/empire of God appreciates the inspiration of the past.
2. The kingdom/empire of God transforms evil.
3. The power of God's kingdom/empire manifests itself in weakness.

Facet Three: Use the Sabbath to benefit human beings.

Facet Four: Trust God to care without first making demands. (Also see Attitude Seven: Facet 2)

Attitude Seven: Replace anxiety with trust.

Facet One: Do not waste your energy on anxiety.

Facet Two: Trust God to care without first making demands. (See Attitude Six: Facet Four.)

Facet Three: Expect basic needs to be met.

1. Expect to be physically nourished.
2. Expect to be healed
3. Expect a generous supply.

Attitude Eight: Take on outreach responsibility.

Facet One: Accept the kindness that is offered on the road.

1. Accept hospitality.
2. Accept meals.

Facet Two: Be prepared for discouragement.

1. Those who know you best will be your harshest judges.
2. Some successes will turn to failure.
3. People will resist change.

Facet Three: Hold firm when your coping skills are challenged.

Facet Four: Stand fast to the demands for going to Jerusalem.

1. Release yourself from the priority of family authority.
2. Create conditions from which kingdom behaviors can emerge unknown to you.

Appendix Two: Questions for Discussion

Laughing with Jesus.

1. Is it hard to think of Jesus as having a sense of humor?
2. Would you like to laugh with him?
3. What do you think of calling his behavior "good trouble?"

Methodology and Purpose.

1. Is the work of the Jesus Seminar scholars encouraging or worrisome?
2. How difficult is it for you to accept the point of view that the Jesus story was written and interpreted decades after he died?
3. Are the reasons given for an attitude approach to Jesus studies sufficiently substantial?

Reference Tool: What did Jesus do?

1. Are there any surprises here for you regarding what Jesus did or did not do?
2. What impresses you about Jesus' activity?
3. Would you have followed Jesus? Why or why not?
4. Do you have a theory about why Jesus was murdered?

Attitude One: Make your life count.

1. To make one's life count, does it help to revere a divine authority?
2. What are the implications of revering a gender specific divinity?
3. How does Jesus compare to newer powers, especially in recent centuries (e.g., medical science, computer science), that have been released into the world?
4. What does it mean to gain life by losing it?

Attitude Two: Practice goal-oriented passion.

1. Where in your experience, secular or sacred, have you seen powerful examples of urgency or passion?
2. What might be the reasons that Jesus would have a sense of urgency?
3. Wherein lies your own greatest sense of urgency?

Attitude Three: Be other-centered in relationships.

1. Is outward behavior the truest measure of who a person is?
2. What actions of protection of self and others can be practiced within this non-vengeful system?
3. Should we think of these attitudes as realism or exaggeration for effect?
4. How do you suppose that one becomes motivated to trust an adversary to be other-centered?
5. What system do you want to change? Discuss a method that Jesus might favor?
6. How is one to respond to someone who denies the need for forgiveness?

Attitude Four: Encourage the powerless.

1. If given the opportunity, how would you attack hunger and poverty?
2. If given the opportunity, how would you attack the sex-trading of children?
3. Is giving without expectation of return realism or exaggeration for effect?

Attitude Five: Use your money for unselfish purposes.

1. How would the world look without a medium of exchange?
2. How does someone you admire manage his/her money?
3. If you are for or against redistributing income, what are your reasons, and how would you make it happen?

4. Can you explain a circumstance or situation where money is or was a corrupting factor?

Attitude Six: Be flexible in the use of tradition.

1. What must gospel scholars do to gain a wider hearing from the public?
2. Jesus' life is now tradition. How can his own attitude be used for or against him?
3. Do you prefer the phrases "God's way" and "ruler's way" to the more history specific terms "God's kingdom/empire" and "Caesar's kingdom/empire?" Why?
4. If the kingdom/empire of God took shape among us, what would it look like?

Attitude Seven: Replace anxiety with trust.

1. Where can one find trust?
2. Can you describe a personal experience where you were able to replace anxiety with trust?
3. Knowing the realities of this life, do we have to trust beyond the grave to find justice?

Attitude Eight: Take on outreach responsibility.

1. What things constitute the biggest resistances to change?
2. In what ways are you independent of your family's views and practices?
3. What scares you about standing up for a cause?

Looking forward.

1. Is it doable to create a society of equals similar to Crossan's description of Jesus' goals?
2. What is compelling for you personally in this 21st century?

3. What is today's equivalent to walking across the country, depending on others for food and lodging, to pursue what is crucial to you?

BIBLIOGRAPHY

Corley, Kathleen E. "Gender and Class in the Teaching of Jesus." In *Profiles of Jesus*, edited by Roy W. Hoover, 137–60. Santa Rosa, California: Polebridge, 2002.

Crossan, John Dominic. *The Essential Jesus: What Jesus Really Taught*. SanFrancisco: HarperCollins, 1994.

_____, Jesus: *A Revolutionary Biography*. New York: HarperCollins, 1995.

Dewey, Arthur J., Hoover, Roy W., McGaughy, Lane C., Schmidt, Daryl D. *The Authentic Letters of Paul: A New Reading of Paul's Rhetoric and Meaning*. Salem, Oregon: Polebridge, 2010.

Ford, Richard Q. "Jesus' Parable of the Talents and the 2008 Olympics." *The FourthR* 21:4 (2008), 13–15, 18–19, 24.

Funk, Robert W. *A Credible Jesus: Fragments of a Vision*. Santa Rosa, California: Polebridge, 2002.

_____, *Honest to Jesus: Jesus for a New Millennium*. SanFrancisco, Harper: Polebridge, 1996.

Funk, Robert W., Hoover, Roy W., and the Jesus Seminar. *The Five Gospels: What Did Jesus Really Say?* New York, Scribner: Polebridge, 1993.

Funk, Robert W. and the Jesus Seminar. *The Acts of Jesus: What Did Jesus Really Do?* SanFrancisco, HarperCollins: Polebridge, 1998.

_____, *The Gospel of Jesus According to the Jesus Seminar*. Santa Rosa, California: Polebridge, 1999.

Goldensen, Robert M., Editor in Chief. *Longman Dictionary of Psychology and Psychiatry*. New York: Longman, 1984.

Hedrick, Charles W. *The Wisdom of Jesus: Between the Sages of Israel and the Apostles of the Church.* Eugene, Oregon: Cascade Books, 2014.

Jackson, Glenna S. "The Woman with the Empty Jar (Thomas 97 and Africa)." *The FourthR* 33:3 (2020), 3, 10.

Keith, Chris. *Jesus Against the Scribal Elite: The Origins of the Conflict.* Grand Rapids, Michigan: Baker Academic, 2014.

Miller, Robert J., ed. *The Complete Gospels: The Scholars' Version*, 4th Ed. Salem, Oregon: Polebridge, 2010.

_____, "Inside(r)s and Outside(r)s: A Question of Boundaries in a Saying of Jesus." *The FourthR* 33:1 (2020), 9–12, 24.

ENDNOTES

[1] Goldenson, *Longman Dictionary of Psychology and Psychiatry*, 71.
[2] Crossan, *The Essential Jesus*, 22.
[3] See, for example, Dewey, et.al., *The Authentic Letters of Paul: A New Reading of Paul's Rhetoric and Meaning*, 17, 72–73, 179, 199.
[4] Miller, *The Complete Gospels*, 20.
[5] Estimates place the ability to read and write in the Jewish State of Jesus time at 3-5% of the population. See Crossan, *Jesus: A Revolutionary Biography*, 25–26.
[6] Funk, *The Acts of Jesus*, 8.
[7] Funk, *The Five Gospels*, ix.
[8] Funk, *The Acts of Jesus*, 26.
[9] Funk, *The Five Gospels*, 28, 30–32, 549–53.
[10] Funk, *The Acts of Jesus*, 566–68.
[11] For summaries, see Funk, *The Acts of Jesus*, 527–34, and *The Five Gospels*, 566–68. See also the individual gospel texts.
[12] Corley, "Gender and Class n the Teachings of Jesus," 157, citing McCane, Byron R., "Let the Dead Bury Their Own Dead: Secondary Burial and Matthew 8:21–22." *Harvard Theological Review* 83 (1990), 38–39.
[13] Corley, "Gender and Class in the Teachings of Jesus," 157.
[14] Funk, *The Acts of Jesus*, 556.
[15] Miller, *The Complete Gospels*, 299.
[16] Funk, *The Acts of Jesus*, 566.
[17] Miller, *The complete Gospels*, 162.
[18] Miller, "Inside(r)s and Outside(r)s: A Question of Boundaries in a Saying of Jesus," 10.
[19] Miller, *The Complete Gospels*, 27.
[20] Miller, *The Complete Gospels*, 151.
[21] Funk, *Honest to Jesus*, 173.
[22] Funk, *Honest to Jesus*, 174–75.
[23] Funk, *Honest to Jesus*, 213–14.
[24] Funk, *The Five Gospels*, 219.

[25] Crossan, *Jesus: A Revolutionary Biography*, 61.
[26] Funk, *Honest to Jesus*, 155, crediting the insights of Walter Wink.
[27] Crossan, *Jesus: A Revolutionary Biography*, 62–64.
[28] Corley, "Gender and Class in the Teachings of Jesus," 149.
[29] Funk, *Honest to Jesus*, 155.
[30] Funk, *Honest to Jesus*, 155.
[31] Funk, *The Acts of Jesus*, 523.
[32] Miller, *The Complete Gospels*, 111.
[33] Ford, "Jesus' Parable of the Talents and the 2008 Olympics," 13–15, 18–19, 24.
[34] Keith, *Jesus Against the Scribal Elite*, 15–38.
[35] A minority of Jesus Seminar scholars have concluded that the phrase "Kingdom of God/Empire of God" originated with the early church rather than with Jesus. For a detailed explanation see Hedrick, *The Wisdom of Jesus*, 134–35.
[36] Funk, *The Gospel of Jesus*, 101.
[37] Jackson, "The Woman with the Empty Jar (Thomas 97 and Africa)," 3.
[38] Crossan, *Jesus: A Revolutionary Biography*, 97–101.

Made in the USA
Columbia, SC
27 October 2020